The Potential of Real Estate Rentals

Table of Contents

Introduction

It is everyone's desire to pursue an avenue that generates income that helps them achieve financial freedom. This is by reaching a position where one is able to create a stream of sources of cash flow that he no longer worries about the cost of living.

Passive income can be a good way of attaining this goal. It entails making investments that start returning income on a regular basis. The effort and time in creating the investment is upfront, and once the investment is set up, it no longer requires time or effort. Passive income, therefore, makes a person free and creates the time for people to live life assured of income without having to work.

The appeal of this income the freedom that is associated with it. Everyone who hates the exhaustion of active income and how it takes up time will obviously enjoy the relief of passive income. It ensures that one does not worry about the days when they may be unable to work as well as prepares one well for retirement.

With passive income, one does not always require huge capital to invest. This is because there are so many opportunities available nowadays for passive income. They suit both those who are seasoned in investment as well as beginners desiring to plunge into the investment world.

Investment in the rentals sector can be a viable avenue to create a stream of regular cash flow. This is because it has a lot of investment specialties that suit people of varied capital potentials. Those who have big money can invest as property owners. However, collaborations are also possible to give anyone interested in the sector to invest and create an opportunity for income.

This book, therefore, describes how income can be expanded for investment purposes. It comes to instigate urgency towards investment and portray the possibilities that await those who can dare them. It targets seasoned investors to show how best to maximize rents and open them to new opportunities in the real estate sector. It also targets those who are yet to realize the need to invest early. It portrays the dangers of depending on active income and impresses on them to get out and realize they can achieve a lot with investment.

Chapter : 1
Compound Interest and Its Advantages

Making money is fun, but investing it needs a lot of discipline. Understanding what methods you can use to increase your income is one of the best ways to gain financial freedom. Compound interest is one strategy that can help you achieve success faster, albeit with small capital.

One great advantage of compound interest is that it works for every investor, including those in the real estate business. In this chapter, we look at several aspects associated with the compound interest investment strategy, including the definition, advantages, and some tips you need to succeed in compound interest.

What is Compound Interest?

By definition, compound interest is the interest derived on both the principal and accrued interest of investment. It is an act of postponing of any short term financial gratification so as to earn profit from it in the long run. In other words, it is when your investment and any interest earned from it continue to give you more interest. No wonder it is referred to as the eighth wonder of the world.

3

Compound interest is also known as compound growth and works fairly in real estate the same way it works with loans or shares. The main focus of every real estate businessperson is to achieve financial stability. The business of buying and selling a property is a good way to make money. When compound interest is incorporated in it, the returns are simply amazing.

When it comes to investment, two types of interest are involved. Simple interest and compound interest. Simple interest is more common, and there is a very huge difference between the two. Compound interest is based on recurring payment calculations that are added to the principal amount at the end of each compounding period. Simple interest, on the other hand, is derived from the principal amount and does not generate recurring interest. Most investors go for compound interest because it helps them gain wealth faster than simple interest. Compound interest benefits can be earned daily, monthly, or yearly depending on your investment terms. Although some companies will apply the interest based on different attributes such as the average daily account balance of the balance on a certain date of the month.

Compound Interest and Real Estate

In terms of real estate, compound interest means that an individual's investment in a property or asset is bringing him more money. Interest made from an asset over the years can be invested in more properties, and this will increment over time as the property's value increases. To help you understand this concept better, let us assume that your income from a property is exactly the same as your expenses. This means that there is neither negative nor positive cash flow from this investment. However, history shows that with time, this property will appreciate in value. If the value grows high by let's say 3% a year, the property will be worth millions more after a good number of years. At this stage, if you acquired the property via a mortgage, you would have paid off the debt and maybe started getting some good income from the property.

One major advantage of compounding interest in real estate is that the longer you investor retains a property or asset, the more profit you make. It is for this purpose that most property owners take years, and even decades before trading their assets. This is also the reason why millions and millions of people join the real estate business every day. Compounding real estate benefits can help you purchase more properties or assets without having to raise the required capital since the accrued interest will be increasing as time goes by.

Compound Interest and Reinvesting Profits

In case you would want to manage your investment profits better, compound interest is one of the best ways to achieve this. Compounding your profits is the same as reinvesting them. However, this may fail to be true in case you have debt because in most cases, the interest will also be deducted on compounding terms.

As discussed earlier, compound interest comes from a principal amount and the interest resulting from it. Repeated cycles of the compounding process often yield exponential growth in terms of profit. For example, if you deposit $1000 in a bank account at an interest of 10% in a year, you will have $1100 at the end of the first year. If you do not claim your interest, this amount will be used as the principal for the second year. At the end of the second year, you will have a total of $1210 in the account. A continuous cycle of this is what brings about the rapid growth that is absent in the simple interest concept. You can learn more about this from the table below.

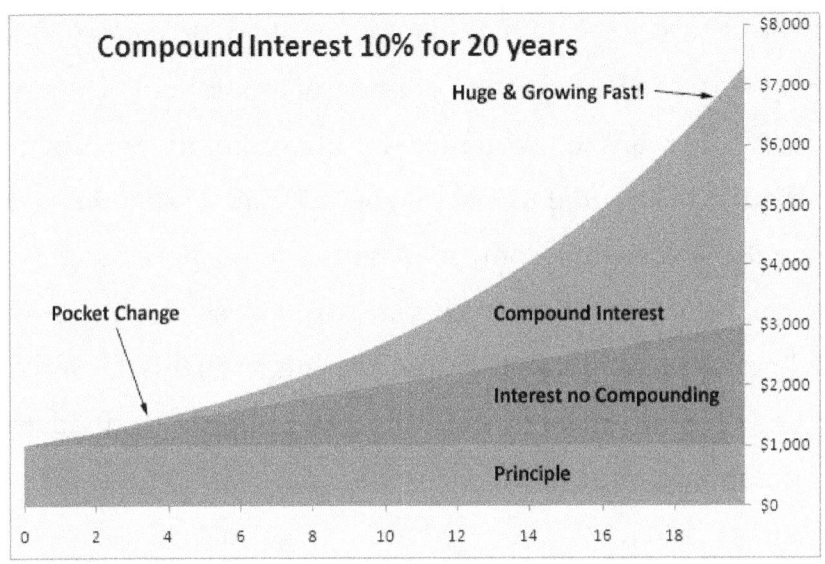

Table 1.0: 20-year compound interest at 10% for a principal amount of $1000

Certainly, this tells you that it is impossible for compound interest to work on borrowed money. The reason is obvious. You will spend most of the interest repaying the loan. Eventually, you may end up without any interest or may keep reducing the principal amount, thus closing the account.

Compound Interest Formula

This is not as easy as calculating simple interest. However, with the right information at hand, it becomes quite straightforward to derive master and apply the underlying compound interest formula.

Before you start thinking about compounding your money, make sure you have a rough estimate of the amount of interest you would want to accumulate by the end of the investment period. It is essential to make some calculated estimations, as you also incorporate some possibilities to see how much you can make or lose in each scenario. Most investors make use of online calculators as well as spreadsheets to do this. However, it is better to analyze the numbers critically and do the calculations yourself.

You can utilize the formula below to calculate your compound interest.

$$A = P (1 + [r / n]) \char`\^ nt$$

Whereby:

A stands for the total amount of money that you will end up with after the interest. In other words, this is the principal plus a total sum of the interest you will earn after the compounding period.

P stands for the principal amount invested

N is the compounding frequency that the interest will be calculated in each year

r refers to the interest rate, normally computed annually

t is the number of years

Please note that this formula's result is the future value of your investment or capital It is a sum of the principal and the interest. If you would like to obtain the interest only, subtract the principal from the result. Therefore, for the interest only the formula will be:

$$A = [P (1 + [r / n]) \wedge nt] - P$$

For example, if an investor deposits $5000 into an account at an interest of 5% compounded on a monthly basis. The interest rate after 10 years will be:

$$A = [5000(1+0.05/12) \wedge 120] - 5000$$

This comes to $3235 in 10 years.

The Importance of Controlling Your Interests

Any time one mentions about interest, we often think of a loan or debt. However, compound interest is not about debts. It is a concept that allows you to grow your money besides just having it in a savings account.

Real estate investors do not make profits overnight. Yet the real estate industry is one of the best in terms of assured profits. Most people are into real estate just for the purpose of making money; however, the benefits of engaging in the business are quite several. Some of these include:

- The ability to build equity for the future
- Passive income that may be tax-free
- The advantage of owning physical assets and
- The fact that real estate appreciates over time

The good side is, the cash flow that is obtained from real estate is always good. The bad side may arise if investors do not engage in a solid reinvestment strategy.

It is true that if you make an investment and leave it untouched for several years, you can gain a lot of money out of it, without having to top up the principal amount. This can never be true if you do not have any money to generate interest from. Compound interest comes from what you have invested, not what you have spent.

As an investor, if you learn to maintain ownership of your asset, you will eventually enjoy the exponential growth of your finances.

Besides the exponential growth of your interests, here are some important facts that you need to know about compound interest before choosing it as a reinvestment strategy.

- *Anyone can gain from it* – Whether you are in real estate or any other type of business, you can still benefit from compound interest if you plan your investments carefully. The strategy can only turn against you if you are a person of debts. It is not a strategy for the rich either. The compounding terms work for $50 the same way they would for $100,000. Although any amount is acceptable for compounding, understand that you can earn better amounts from compound interest if you invest a huge sum of money.

- *The higher the compounding frequency, the higher the gain* - To grow your interests faster, you will need to save as often as you can. For instance, it is better for your profits to be compounded monthly or quarterly than when done annually.

- *Time is the essence* – the longer the compounding period the better. Interest that is compounded at a rate of 6% will give you double within 12 years. However, if this is left for 24 years it will give you four times as much.

- *Growth is Exponential* – as stated earlier, compound interest accumulates faster than you can ever imagine. If you are able to save just $5 every month at 5% interest, you would end up with approximately $600 in your possession after 10 months. To achieve this, however, you must make consistent deposits and sacrifice a few luxuries. In most cases, the end gain is greater than the little amount you sacrifice to save.

Since compound interest is based on the interest that is already paid to you, it means that you can make a good amount of cash just from having a principal deposit in your account. It is a kind of investment where all you do is invest some amount in your account and leave it to continuously make interest without doing anything.

Compound Interest as a Long-term Strategy

Unlike other investments that create profit within days, compound interest may fail to give you a lot of gain in the first few days, or months. This applies mostly where the principal amount is very little since the profits realized within the first few compounding periods may be significantly small.

Compound interest in itself is a long-term investment strategy. You must be able to allow your interests to accumulate over a good period of time for you to realize all the benefits. The first few interest cycles may fail to be impressive, especially when the interest rate is quite low. However as time goes by and the interest continues to add up, you will easily notice a positive change in your account balance.

You can choose this method for your long-term investment purposes. Compounding is good both for young and experienced real estate investors. The concept of compound interest requires patience. It may fail to work for those who are in a rush to make quick money. The more you invest, the more you earn. This is an important point to note for young investors who may get discouraged because of the slow compounding process. One great motivation about this strategy is that the interest doesn't grow at a steady rate, it grows exponentially since the more you earn, the more your principal amount grows.

To benefit from this strategy, you must first learn how to control your cash flow, or rather your interests. It does not matter whether you are making small or big profits. What matters is that something, however small, has been set aside for reinvesting.

When you get to controlling and reinvesting your interest, there are four major things that you should always bear in mind.

1. Reinvesting your interests is one great way to grow. It allows you to maximize your savings. The more time you allow for growth, the more your interest accumulates. Saving your money in a bank account

that does not generate any interest means missing an opportunity to multiply your money

2. How soon you put your money into it determines how fast it starts compounding. With compounding interest, the earlier the better since the most important variable here is time. By applying interest rates on your principal amount several times and several times, the result is only one – increased profits.

3. Taking huge risks can result in a tremendous loss of your capital. This will, in turn, reduce the number of benefits that you would have received from compounding your interests.

4. Every dollar spent today is a lost opportunity tomorrow. When it comes to compound growth, each dollar you spend now would have generated a lot more in the future if you invested it instead.

Compounding Period

The compounding period refers to the number of times your interest is compounded. It can be once, twice or several times a year. Note that the more frequent your interest is compounded the faster your returns grow. This is due to the fact that each computation is done depending on the most previous account balance.

The compounding period depends on what is called the compounding frequency. This can be defined as the number of times that the interest is accrued to the investor. The higher the compounding frequency the more the interest. The lower the frequency the lower the interest. For instance, $200 compounded at 5% annually will accumulate more interest than if the same amount is compounded at 10% per annum.

Have a look at the table below to see how changes in the compounding period can affect your interests.

Compounding Frequency	Number of Compounding Periods	End-of-Period Balance
Annually	1	$2,594
Quarterly	4	$2,685
Monthly	12	$2,707
Daily	365	$2,718

Table 2.0: Shows the difference in computation period for the same principal amount

Source: calculatorsoup.com.

From table 2.0 above, you can quickly notice the difference in interest for each compounding period. For example, the difference between quarterly and annual compounding is a whopping $91. From this, you are able to conclude that how frequent your interest is compounded really matters. Also, how long the computations are left to recur is what determines if your money will grow or not. Be sure to check the interest rate as well since higher rates will mean that your investment will accumulate interest at a faster rate.

This illustration helps you to understand that there is no shortcut to building your investment portfolio then investing more for longer periods. It even becomes a lot easier when you understand the place of patience and time in the whole process.

Advantages of Compounding on Long term

Generally, there are two types of investors. One that times the market and makes short term gain and another one that creates a long-term investment strategy. One great advantage of compounding in the long term is that it becomes easier to predict the market accurately. This is not the case with short-term investments. Another great advantage is the cost involved, especially in real estate. Every time you sell a property or asset, there is a cost involved in terms of the transaction fees and commissions in the case where brokers are involved. Waiting for a long time to trade an asset means fewer transactions, and this translates to fewer costs.

Compounding and the Rule of 72

The Rule of 72 is a useful formula that you can use to estimate the amount of time and percentage rate required to double your investments over a certain period of time. This rule is ideal when drafting your compounding goals as it can help you determine what you need to transform your capital into a large financial fortune.

The rule states that if you divide 72 by the annual rate of investment, you will get the number of years required for your investment to double. For example, investing $500 for an annual interest of 20% becomes %1000 in 3.6 years since 72 divide by 20 is 3.6. This rule can be used by investors to see how powerful compounding is and make them appreciate the benefits of making long-term investment plans.

Why Reinvest Your Capital Gain?

In real estate, there is capital, and there is capital gain. Capital gain refers to the difference between an asset's purchase cost and its worth during its time of sale. This can either be short term or long term.

If you own an asset or property that is consistently appreciating in value, your interest will keep growing in addition to the capital invested in it. Looking at real estate keenly, most of the profit is from:

1. The building or property appreciating in value, then sold at a profit
2. The investor may rent the property out for an amount that is higher than the expenses incurred; this becomes a steady cash flow to the investor

This profit is what can be turned into a fortune through compound interest. Sadly, in many instances, investors tend to spend all the profit on things that are of no profit. This is particularly common in inexperienced investors, yet it's not a good practice because once you spend the returns, you do not have any hope of growing interests from your business.

Any profitable business must always have long-term sustainability plans in mind. That is why it's important to use your profits to expand your investments. Remember, each investment is an opportunity to grow. If you do not invest, you cease to grow. Things become even more difficult when asset prices go down. At this point, if you do not have an investment to turn to, things may get really tough.

Most investors utilize all their income for mortgage repayments. By doing this, they do not get to benefit from compound interest. One great thing about property is that the cost keeps rising each year. This means that each consecutive year adds a percentage to your interest base. In this case, for example, a property that costs $200,000 may grow at 5% annually. After ten years, the same property will be worth $325,000. If the interest rate increases, then the investor may end up with double the cost price after the same period elapses. No wonder the real estate industry keeps attracting millions of investors every single day.

Utilizing all your capital gain leaves you without any assurance for long-term investment. One way of ensuring your real estate business operates smoothly is by increasing the efficiency with which money comes in. Without an investment plan, you may not have the required financial ability to deal with any emergencies that may arise. Once your business starts generating an income, it is important that you start thinking about ways through which you can multiply your earnings. Remember, the more you hold on your property, the higher its value becomes. This is one of the easiest ways to accumulate wealth in the real estate industry.

One reason why you should not spend all your profits is that you will be able to fund your business growth by yourself. This will ensure that you remain debt-free and you will remain in full charge of your business. It is always complicated to get outside investors, partners, or creditors to fund your business. Involving such people grants them a certain level of influence in the way the business is run. Eventually, if you are not careful, you may end up losing the business to outsiders. To avoid all this, always have a reinvestment plan for your profits.

Ultimately, saving your capital gain in an interest-generating account is better than putting it aside just for the sake of it. In seeking to grow capital gains, most people often think of reinvesting their earnings. A good number, however, do not figure out how to do so in a way that protects their income as much as possible. Rolling your capital gains to another investment can help you diversify your financial portfolio, thus minimize your investments' overall risk and exposure. For instance, if you have gained some profit from selling a property, you can reduce your tax by reinvesting this in another property.

To achieve this, here are some practical tips that will ensure that you keep growing your capital gains into more profit.

Have a Goal

The initial step in reinvesting your real estate profits is setting a goal. This can be in terms of the expected income, or the timelines. For instance, you may define your annual interest goal of $20,000 from your investment profits. Using this figure, you will be able to determine how much you need to accumulate in order to earn $20,000 from it. You will also be able to tell the number of months or years you need to do the compounding, and at what interest rate.

Start Small

Of course, it is always good to invest, however small. If you can invest small amounts on a regular basis, you will have some good interest over time. This is due to the compounding effect that applies to your latest balance to compute the interest. Even if your goal is a long-term one, it is important to start saving early. The earlier you begin, the more time you will have for your interest to grow.

Increase the Compounding Frequency

Once you have your interest goals defined, find out how much you will need to accumulate to achieve your goal. In compound growth, time is of the essence. Start saving early to avoid the issue of having to part with large deposits each month. You can keep reducing your deposits as the interests grow.

Choose your Reinvestments Wisely

The interest you get on your investments plays a big role in determining how fast your money grows. Having this in mind, it is important to ensure that whatever deal you are investing in is the best. If it is a property, make a comparison of the available properties and establish how this can be of benefit to you in the long-term before putting your interests in it. Check on a regular basis to see how it's performing and make sure you balance between the potential of growth and risk tolerance.

Avoid debts

One unfortunate truth about compound interest is that it can work against you in case of debt. If you have a loan, the interest will be charged on compounding terms, and this only means that you will never be able to accumulate any wealth until your debts are cleared. Before thinking about reinvesting your profits, ensure that you have a strategy in place to clear any pending debts, faster. You might as well negotiate with your creditors to see whether the interest rates can be revised in your favor. One attribute that can make compound interest successful is when you reduce your debts as you save what you can.

Generally, compound interest can go a long way in giving real estate investors their financial freedom. Of course, this is only true when you are the one receiving the interest, not the other way round — understanding how it compounding work can help you move steps ahead in your personal finances. The key lies in starting early, even if it means starting small. It is better to make repeated small deposits when you can than wait to make one large deposit later, as this may never happen. In the long run, you will have accumulated enough interest that you can decide to reinvest or utilize to accomplish your financial goals.

Chapter : 2
Understanding Passive Income

In recent times, anxiety has gripped a lot of people over their financial planning as they prepare for life presently and the future. This is due to the consumer lifestyles that people are adopting in the current era. This anxiety has pushed people to pursue any avenues that can stream in income to finance their immediate needs as well as their later life. Passive income, however, particularly serves the needs of the middle-aged generations and younger. This is the proverbial wannabe generation that aspires to live fancy lifestyles but has not grown up with the character of hard work and zeal. They therefore always scout for money-making avenues that guarantee maximum profits with a minimum of effort required as possible.

With the advent of the internet and technology, opportunities to engage in passive occupations have multiplied. These opportunities are varied in nature and promise an income for those who engage in them. For instance, there have been online marketing websites that pay people for viewing ads on their smartphones. These online sites usually target online users who spent a better part of their time online. Various companies realize that this is an opportunity for digital marketing of their products and have hence created a platform for potential consumers of their products to be motivated for just viewing their products. This is in the hope of popularizing the products and daring viewers to buy them.

There are other similar opportunities online too that offer similar opportunities for relaxed work that guarantee a constant income. This includes participation in online surveys that are created by various companies to gather data on the fan base to inform their structure of designing products. Other digital avenues of passive income are in the form of crypto exchanges that have quickly been gaining pace in the course of the current decade.

It is not enough to describe the popularity of passive income to just the more technologically conversant generations. It also arises from the very economic circumstances that have confronted people for a long time. From instance, having automatic income may not customarily take care of all the kinds of expense that may arise in the period before the next earning. This may include funerals, car servicing, medical bills, and other expenses that come with being a family and community member. This exerts a lot of pressure on the salary that is also required for savings to cater for pension years, development plans, and overall daily needs.

Even for the generation of baby boomers report finding it difficult to survive just on the savings that they made in the active years of work. It appears like the saving structure of the old is no longer guaranteeing that one will live their life comfortably in retirement. Governments are also continuing to cut expenditures and as such, even retirement years in order to merit pension have been raised. This is in an era where the overall life expectancy has dropped to an average of 45 years. Even if people were assured of longevity, it is not comfortable to work the entire length to stipulated retirement age. As a matter of fact, it defeats any logic to have to work more years to be subjected to higher taxation and in return get a pension that may just not be commensurate with the labor and service.

Passive income comes in to grant one the much-needed cash flow that does not come with the automatic income. In this case, there is always some drop of a coin in the pocket at a determined span of time, which is akin to enrolled employment that comes with a paycheck. The exception, in this case, is that one is not in active work as is with a normal regular occupation.

This usually assures someone and gives them relief from the pressure of work. When there is no alternative income, one is restrained to continuous work even when they may be sick. One has the pressure to keep working even to overtime and can decline taking leaves. However, a passive income relaxes a person, and they can take leaves on discretion since there is always an income that is assured. One is, therefore, better able to schedule expenditures and can dispatch any arising emergencies in the interval before they earn without anxiety.

Passive Income Comes with Taxation Benefits

One of the things known about wealthy people is that they enjoy flexible on taxes for the various forms of income that flows in. Different forms of income are not subjected to similar taxation systems. In the best case scenario, passive income can be exposed to very low taxation or the tax can be imposed on a date later. In isolated cases, some passive incomes are not subjected to taxation at all. The common trend is usually for active income to involve the highest tax rates with unguaranteed reliefs if any at all.

The reason why passive income is not as much taxed is that it involves some level of complexity. Usually, one only needs to key in a certain value to represent the period being taxed and another value for the amount of money under taxation. The determined formula of taxation imposes it at Z rate, and this will chop off the corresponding portion of the earning. This is straight forward.

On the other hand, passive incomes sometimes can be too remote even to be mapped out by the taxation authorities. The earnings may not even be found within the existing taxation laws to be subjected to the same. They are outside of the taxation radar and sometimes defeat international monetary regulations which benefit those who are involved in it. Looking at passive income relative to active income leads to the conclusion that in fact, passive income is better and scores higher on the taxation test.

Create Streams of Passive Incomes from One

Some forms of Passive income usually involve effort that is exerted ahead of the pay. Time is also invested upfront, and afterward, the entire venture can be left to run and still bring in earnings. This is where the passiveness of it sets in. Afterward, one can take some money from the earnings and channel it into another venture that does not involve a high risk but can bring in good returns. If one builds a blog, for example, it will take a lot of time and effort at the onset before earnings can start to stream in. Afterward, the builder of the blog sits tight to earn commissions as the blog swings into use. This will run for a long time, and the earnings can be channel into another such venture to lead to a stream of income ventures that guarantee income. The advantage is that, after pumping in a lot of time and effort upfront, the venture will not require similar rigor once it is operational and working.

Improving Quality of Life

It is useless to engage in passive income that does not show in the quality of life of a person. Good enough, this is a promise that is usually delivered with this form of income. With a better quality of life, it is not to denote that one is idle and free and that they can travel as they like. Instead, one could enjoy a better state of health and can have a better opportunity to build relations. This is because regular work is in itself a stressor and the fact that the earnings are not sufficient compounds. This boils up into emotional disturbance and eventually infiltrates the interactions in society and family. With the pressure of work, one cares less about such things as what they eat and do not bother with exercise and other lifestyle aspects that indicate the quality of life. With passive income, one finds themselves freed up and to focus adequately on the things, in life fully, that really matter.

The bottom line is that passive income comes in handy to bolster self-development. This can show physically through the various property acquisitions that can be made possible. It can also help emotionally by granting one the peace, time, and the rare opportunity to feel pay attention to one's own life other than the call of duty in active income. Besides, it is a good avenue when one is pursuing financial freedom, which aspect will be discussed in greater length in this book. The cash flow that comes can also boost one's regular income and help one slow down with work pre-occupations.

Of essence is the fact that I passive income, there is the aspect of automation. This is because of the upfront effort and investment of time to build a system that then runs like a clock while reaping dividends. This, however, does not mean that passive income is totally hands-off and that one lives to pile up sacks of money without any effort at all. It still calls for discipline and regular checking of the systems to ensure they continue to guarantee earnings. Passive income is creating the bigger system and its framework with the details that require daily work automated to guarantee the investor regular, meaningful returns.

Financial Freedom

Life in the modern world is understood in the financial sense. This measures the worth of individuals, countries, and corporate entities. This is what drives people into work. It is as if the lack of financial worth could spell the end of life. The struggle for financial sufficiency has therefore turned into a struggle for survival. Those who have conquered this attain financial freedom. Financial freedom in this regard measures the value of one's regular earnings minus the expenses for every month. Sometimes calculating financial freedom takes having to multiply one's annual expenses by twenty-five (25). The resultant is then compared with the accumulated savings for the said year. Finding that the annual expenses are lesser than the accumulated savings is an indicator of attainment of financial freedom.

In this sense, financial freedom denotes the ability of one to use their regular earnings to meet their month by month expenses as well as save. These expenses include the emergent ones that may be unforeseen in the course of financial planning. Upon attainment of financial freedom, one can be able to exercise their whims and impulses without experiencing much strain. It also comes with a high level of risk tolerance. This means that a person does not get completely blown out in case of experiencing certain losses or setbacks that entail financial implications.

In understanding financial freedom, money is taken as a means to an end. The end of the general is living a good life that is near without limits. One is particularly able to meet the essentials of life for themselves and dependents. He can also fend for the needs of dependents but also manages to acquire luxuries that bequeath someone status and comfort in life.

The word freedom is of the essence in this regard. Freedom is about making life easier for one's self. It is freedom from work. Everyone has the natural instinct to avoid work and wish there was an easier way out to achieve their ends without having to labor much. It is also freedom from worry and anxiety. This emanates from living unsure of what happens tomorrow since one is not in control of things in their life. For instance, when one has a debt to service, pending bills and other obligations for which he has limited ability to dispatch. As it is, freedom is about discretion and whims. That one is free to do as they please, whenever, wherever and however.

To live a good life comes with certain costs that become expenses. These expenses are majorly financial. This is the reason why the compensation for labor is financial. They are financial in order that the person who is earning can be able to meet the cost of living the life they desire. If life costs, that, in this regard, are financial, people would not bother to work or get out in pursuit of income.

Those looking for financial freedom are those aspiring for such a life that they can surmount the costs obstacle to a good life. Asking people randomly on how they would live their life if they had all the money they required for life, they would relate their desire for a life that is enviable. A life where they have an opportunity to actualize their dreams and even fantasies and therefore realize the best that they can be in their mental and physical states of being. This includes having to explore the world and experience the best of the world phenomena. This, however, begs the question of the interrelationship between money and happiness. It is worth pondering whether attainment of financial freedom is an express pointer to achieving happiness in life. This is a complicated subject given that some of the people who in the eyes of many have attained financial success still have to grapple with other issues in their lives. These issues include stress, being at odds with various government policies and pressure to sustain the high profile status and keep one's accounts afloat. Besides, some also struggle with relationship problems, health, and addictions that may be destructive. This is not to dismiss the fact that financial freedom helps one to be able to access some of the best amenities and services that bring happiness. However, it can also be a precipitate of overindulgence that can fuel negative behavioral practices that could still prove of great detriment to happiness in life.

It is, therefore, irrelevant to view financial freedom as the only route to happiness in life. It will mean that happiness is a reserve of those who can earn big money only, which is not the case. Financial freedom only increases the purchasing power of an individual. However, happiness is such an amorphous an indecipherable phenomenon that even the richest person cannot claim to be able to afford by merely having dollar-piles in the account. The question then is whether only those who are earning big money can attain financial freedom. Analyzing this question should reveal some of the strategies by which people, on the whole, even those operating on slimmer salaries can realize financial freedom. Financial freedom, in this case, to mean that a person's expenses are lower than their regular earnings.

The Path to Financial Freedom

Financial freedom should be perceived as a destination that many people are journeying to. This is through their various activities that they engage in to earn money and how the earnings are expended. As of any journey, one has to know the exact route, its nature, and how best to prepare in order to navigate it. For instance, this journey to financial freedom involves terminals and checkpoints of various kinds. These are savings, needs, wants, and bullshit.

Savings are essential since people have to try and ensure their future and guarantee themselves a life in the days when their energies start to dwindle. Savings can be done for the sake of preparation to undertake a major project and expand one's net worth or simply for the person of catering for the pensioner years. Savings should be done on a regular pattern and should be a default part of a person's financial system. It should be done automatically and intentionally. Saving usually entails in it the notion of deferment. This is to put forward the satisfaction of certain current needs to a later date. It can be a sacrifice particular for those earning moderate salaries. In as much as it is automatic, it should equally be intentional and tailored towards a certain predetermined goal. It should not be a waste of time and a deprivation of gratification today without a return in the future.

The second aspect is mapping out needs in one's life. Needs hold in them an obligatory undertone. This means that they are essential for life and hence must be satisfied. They cannot be foregone as doing so can take a toll on the quality of life that a person is living. They include the aspect of food, healthcare, shelter, water, and clothing, among other essential needs that simply have got to be satisfied. Understanding needs is essential because if the needs are too costly, they may impact on one's ability to save and dictate the quality of life. In a situation where needs can consume most of the earnings, it becomes difficult to work out a way to attend to other obligations that are part of the journey to financial freedom. Earnings have to surpass one's needs a few times in order to be able to work out a way to guarantee one's self of financial freedom.

Wants also have to be understood. These are things that only satisfy the desire for prestige and luxury. These ones also have to be factored in the expenditure in order to be able to exercise one's desires for a good life. Yet the things that most guarantees comfort and point to achieving a good quality of life fall in the category of wants. They are the ones that most motivate people to desire to achieve financial freedom. In order that one can do as they want, be free to desire and get, one should have the earnings that are not constricted.

The other aspect is to know how to handle liabilities. This is vital, particularly when it comes to debt. One cannot be able to pursue financial freedom if they are perpetually held back by debt. For low-income earners, it does not only exert pressure on one's earnings but also affects the purchasing power of a person. Debts should only be those that are reimbursing an investment borrowing that will ensure that one does not suffer a loss. Any other forms of debt are a liability and totally an obstacle on the journey to financial freedom.

The discourse here is, therefore, positing that financial freedom entails getting rid of debt, ensuring that saving is done automatically, making investments, and raising up one's earnings. In building up the impetus to financial freedom, expenditures should be kept at the lowest possible level. This will help to boost one's net worth. Acquisition of luxuries or wants should be done reasonably as not to fleece one's earnings. This will help to guarantee a state of constant growth and development. The idea is to ensure that efforts that go into income generation have a worth and do not go wasted through reckless spending. Watching expenses until ones net worth has grown is paramount, and saving should be purposeful and targeted. No savings should be done for the sake of it since it will only be wastage and a worthless deferment of gratification.

The Relationship between Automatic Income, Monthly Expenses, and Financial Freedom

Automatic income is a goal that everyone pursuing financial freedom should aspire for. Automatic income in this is not by active work as such. It is the various engagements and investments that one makes that once set, on their own start reaping back financial returns. The logic behind the need for automatic income is that one can be rendered unable to work if they rely on regular work or employment. This should not mean that life then takes a U-turn for the worse. One should have ensured they have set their financial structures such that there is cash flow. This can be in the form of dividends that emanate from shares in financial institutions, passive income, or an entrepreneurial venture. However, this is a difficult goal for many, and only very few achieve it eventually. The capital, time, and effort toll it takes sometimes proves prohibitive. Yet the expenses that people incur in their daily life keep beckoning to be serviced day by day.

The expenses of life have to be beaten if life has to become more interesting. However, it is dangerous to live totally from the salary that comes from active work. The US is one of the countries in the world where consumer debt is high. This is when people particularly those reliant on salaries, have to borrow to meet expenses as opposed to investing. When one's income has risen beyond the earnings that one registers, life becomes full of constraints. It is as if one is surviving as opposed to living. Sometimes, it can even turn into a life on the run. This is because a person starts to live with their breath held, and they cannot for a moment is free of the money factor that is determining their next move. It is an indicator to enslavement and overdependence on work if one lives from the paycheck of one month to the paycheck of another. It is also a total show of being overburdened by expenses since one is unable to invest in other sources of income that can then become automatic income.

In the same vein, it is necessary to realize a poverty threshold that is low. This refers to the average finances that a person requires in a year in order for them to live a life that they feel is enjoyable and interesting. This runs in the same vein as the reduction of expenses. When one's poverty threshold is low, it means that they can be happy with a life that does not involve too much luxury, consumption, and conveniences. Instead of high-end vehicles, one is okay with a second-hand vehicle that is not of premium status. The question pegged under this is whether one would still keep going and be happy with their savings are taken away and the income cut by 80%. If one would be totally miserable and dejected, it is a pointer to a life of high consumption, and this is a psychological metric.

To build a poverty threshold that is low requires self-discipline and accustoming oneself to a life of sacrifice. It is trying as much as possible to, for a certain period, not spend any money. For a month, take the commuter train as opposed to going to the city and paying for fuel and parking fees. On travel, lodge in hostels and shun the urge to check in nice hotels. The point, in this case, is allowing oneself to experience the regular life. The life that would typically be called poor. Taking this life to just fine encourages one to change their minds about life and impacts on their poverty threshold levels.

For the middle-level earner, it also helps to achieve financial freedom if one learns how to master their desires and wants. It can be really stressful if lusts and the unending human wants are left to dominate impulses. Studies have even established that happiness is not directly related to financial well-being at least beyond a certain optimum level. The point here is not to disparage having a lot of money. However, it is to say that the war of financial freedom is fought from both edges. It is about building as much cash flow as to be enough to fend for one's needs without necessarily having to work. But it is also about creating a healthy mental system that is not obsessed with desire.

With modesty in our consumer instinct, it is possible to expand our net worth. We are able to save more and be easily gratified. The urge to make money should not be out-competed by the urge to spend it. One has to at least be under control. Outside of that, even the person who makes the most money becomes the servant of their own possessions as opposed to the possessions serving them. It will be an infinite fallacy to imagine that all that financial freedom is about is making money without reflecting on our financial practices. Reckless habits include assuming that something is only worthy if it is premium. That once there is a stream of cash flow, one does not care about the price-tag. A budget is vital, and monitoring the limits of spending is an essential part of financial freedom.

Chapter : 3
Rental Real Estate Investment as Passive Income

There is a huge difference when it comes to passive and active income in real estate. For most people, the thought of passive income brings to mind the life of sitting back, doing nothing and waiting for the money to come in, which is a wrong assumption as we shall see later in the chapter.

There are various investments that can give you passive income in real estate. One of the top ones is rental income. Rental income entails the type of income that you get every month when you have rental properties that you let.

So, is rental income an active or passive? Before we consider this, we need to first look at what the terms active and passive incomes mean.

Active Income

Active income is the income that you earn when you work on an investment in a continuous and regular basis. On the other hand, passive income arises from an approach that is more of hands-off.

- Active activities include wages, salaries and commission income
- Dividends and interest
- Guaranteed payments
- Bonds and stocks
- Sale of investment property that is undeveloped
- Partnerships where you participate
- Royalties from your businesses

Passive Income

Passive income is the money that comes from investments, but the condition has to be that you don't participate materially in the investment.

An example of passive income is when you invest in property purchase and development, and you receive a percentage of the profit each month. This is passive when you don't participate in the running of the property in any meaningful way.

Is Rental Income Active or Passive?

This is one of the major questions that investors ask when they get into the rental investment market.

Rental income refers to money that you receive for the use of a property. All the rental activities are categorized as passive income. The basis behind this is that you are generating revenue out of money that you have put up for a property. It doesn't matter whether you are acting as the landlord or you have entrusted the property to a property manager – it is still considered passive income.

Due to this, many investors are taking money out of other investments and diverting it to rental properties.

Just like any other investment, you can easily lose money when you invest in rental property. This is why it is vital that you take time to analyze the markets to identify the strong ones so that you can reap the benefits.

According to reports, 97 percent of investors have shown their willingness to divert more funds to real estate investments within the next one and a half years. This shouldn't come as a surprise since you know too well that rental properties come with a lower risk compared to stocks and bonds.

When it comes to rental properties, we have two types of rent – normal rent and short rents. Normal rents are ideal for renting to families, and you are assured of good monthly earnings. However, the rent isn't as high as you would expect it to be. The work to do when you go for normal rent is little, but the returns are good.

On the other hand, short rent comes with high returns, which means they are more profitable than the normal rents. You can use the property for renting out to individuals that stay for a few days then leave. However, the rate of damage is usually high, and you need to make sure you repair the property time and again. You also need to put in a lot of work to make it work for you. Most of the customers for this type of property are tourists.

Why Are Rental Properties So Valuable

So, why are rental properties so valuable to the investors right now? Here are various reasons:

Consistent Rental Income

One of the best aspects of rental properties is that they give you a stable income compared to other investments. You are assured of a paycheck every month, which is a good thing, but the truth is that what you want is to enjoy a positive cash flow property.

Do you know that there are investors who handle rental investments, yet they experience losses? You won't achieve maximum profits when you have a property that gives you low cash flow – what you need it to go for a rental property that gives you positive cash flow.

Hands-off Operation

The element of not being involved in the affairs of the property is one of the best advantages of investing in real estate. As an investor, it is high time that you understand that rental properties have a lot of tasks that you need to work on. The good thing is that there are a lot of management firms that will handle all the tasks on your behalf.

When you wish to enjoy passive income from rental properties, you need to use an investment management company to handle the daily tasks. The tasks include repairs, collecting rent, and even handling disputes.

However, you ought to know that for you to use these services; you need to pay a management fee. This is the major downside of rental properties – you have to spend to get the results you need. You need to add the management fees to the property expenses and then expect them to have an effect on the cash flow. But the expenses aren't too much, and this means you won't be left with anything; you will still maximize your rental income. The good news is that the management company helps to keep the rental fees down as well.

You can Invest Out of State

If you have ever tried to run another property investment, then you need to follow the rules that have been set in the state. Some property investments don't allow you to invest in other states. With rental investments, you aren't restricted to a specific state or location. You can choose to go for a number of locations in other states as long as you know how to choose the property.

When investing in other states, make sure you know whether to opt for short term rentals or long term rentals.

You Invest Part Time

You can run this venture as a part-time investment so that you can still work at your job. It also means you have two streams of income – from your daytime job and the passive income from the rental properties.

However, you shouldn't take this as a guide to think that everything is as easy as it seems. Just because you have a property manager handling the property doesn't give you the opportunity to relax entirely – you have to stay up to fate with the ongoing in the business.

Buying the Best Rental Property for Passive Income

When looking for the best property both within and outside the state, make sure you choose the best one that suits your goals – to make passive income consistently.

The sad thing is that nothing in this life is as easy as it seems – unless you get some advice from an expert. Here are a few expert tips to help you choose the right property for rental income generation.

Research

Just like everything in the market, you need to have knowledge before you can make a decision. This is the same thing with rental income property choice. You have to research each time you choose to go for the purchase, or you wish to sell.

Before you come up with the perfect rental property income strategy, you ought to ask yourself a few questions. These questions need to guide you on what to do, which property to choose, and how to run it.

Once you have a plan, the next thing is to understand what location is best for you to invest on. Before you choose a location, make sure you understand where the market is heading to. Finally, you need to check the local listings and understand the rent per month to expect in a location.

After having a plan, the next step is to make sure you understand the financial implications of your property. For instance, get to understand the funding that you have at your disposal, and how much you expect to make from the whole venture.

Get the Right Financing

You might be very excited when you have a plan in action, but you need to know that for you to start shopping for rental properties, you need to have ready finance. Many people opt to go to the bank to get the finance they need, while many also use their savings.

We talk about finance because acquiring a rental property isn't a simple venture. You need to know that many properties on the market are expensive, and without the right financing, you stand to fail to close the seal.

Have a Plan

Now that you have an idea of the kind of property you need to invest in, the types, location as well as the source of finance, you need to make the plan actionable. Write the plan down on paper and then use the plan as a benchmark for you to achieve your goals.

Identify the Property

This represents the phase that most investors look out for. Here, many people follow their intuition and preferences. It is no different for you, whether a new investor or a seasoned one, you already has an image of the kind of property that you want to invest in. this is the point where you find the property

However, you need to keep in mind that the property you get might not be perfect the way you dream it to be; instead, you have to compromise on a few aspects.

Get Some Help

When getting into real estate investment, it is wise to perform due diligence every time you make a decision. So you feel you have found the right property to invest in, but for your information, nothing always seems to be what it is. This is the stage where you look into some of the negative aspects of the property that might affect your future.

If you are serious about investing in real estate, you need to work with professionals that know what aspects of the building better than you. The professionals approve your assumptions so that you are sure of what you are looking for. They will warn you of the cost issues, the damages and probable problems that might occur later on.

Without taking this step, you are putting your money on the line, and this might end up in losses.

Know When and How Much to Offer

Real estate goes with the seasons. For instance, you find the price low when the demand is low, and the price skyrockets when the demand for properties also goes high. Remember that you can never place a specific price on a rental property – all you can do is to negotiate for the best price ever.

Many traders fail to take emotions into their grasp and end up running for a property that looks glamorous. This is why it is advisable to run away from any property that doesn't fall within your price range. If you learn to walk away from such deals, you will have the upper hand in any negotiation. Remember that if a deal isn't what you expected it to be, you can still get another deal similar to it.

If an offer is near to the final price you plan to sell off the investment in the near future, you need to make sure you look at the associated costs before making the perfect decision.

Make it a Business

Once you close the deal, you need to manage it so that you realize the profits. Rental real estate investments need some sprucing up to do if you plan to make them attractive to tenants.

Work with a post-purchase inspector so that you understand what you need to do to make the property worthy consistent tenants.

Making it Work

Now that you have identified the perfect location for your rental property and you have closed the deal, the next step is to make the whole deal work out. Here are a few tips for doing this.

Maintain a Certain Class

Do you know that if you offer low-end housing, you will definitely end up with low-end tenants? This type of tenants will stress you to the limit, and you will have to hire a management company after another due to the way they behave. The tenants are less likely to submit rent on time or fail to pay the rent altogether. When this happens, you will have to take the tenants to court to force them to pay up.

Another issue is how they handle your property. Remember that the performance of a property is directly related to how it is handled by the tenant. You might end up spending all your gains on repairs and installations.

Many investors think that buying a cheap house is a great find, but this isn't the case at all. How efficient is it when it is always vacant for more than half the year?

You might think that all tenants are responsible and handle the property the right way, but this is just a mirage. Many tenants have come up with ways to hoodwink the system and will go to all lengths to frustrate you.

So, once you choose the right location, make sure you don't invest lower. Instead of looking for deals in the slums, go for middle-class housing that gives you the best passive income.

Screen Your Tenants

If you plan to live on your passive income, you need to lease the property to tenants that are able to pay their rent each time of the month, rather than switch off their mobile phones when you start asking about overdue rent.

When you decide to get tenants for your property, it is advisable that you perform extreme screening. Don't fail to check on their background or credit reports before you can let them into the house. This task is usually best done by the property manager.

The property manager usually called up their employer or supervisor with the main aim of understanding more about the tenant. If you find that the tenant lied about some things, you shouldn't lease the property to them.

Avoid Fast Turnovers

Turnovers translate into more work and expenses. Remember if you are always screening tenants, it means that you have to put in more effort into the property. The solution to this is to go after long term leases. You can have a condition that whoever leases your property takes it for a minimum of a year. The idea is to make sure you have tenants that will help you met your goals without taking your expenses through the roof.

Opt for Retention

The only way you can enjoy a longer retention rate is if you have good tenants. Having good tenants is all about proper seeing (as discussed above).

Always shoot for longer retention periods so that you don't expose your business to risks that you don't expect. If you get a tenant that pays rent on time, then hold onto them.

To do this, you need to make improvements to the property regularly. This encourages tenants to stay for longer, and they will recommend the property to their friends and colleagues. The good thing is that this cost of upgrading the property is tax deductible, which reduces your expenses.

In conclusion, you need to know that passive income doesn't come automatically – you have to come up with a strategy that gives you the best way to identify and grab a property that you desire. Work with professionals that know what you need and help you achieve it. Finally, after you close the deal, make sure you don't incur a lot of costs due to high turnover rates.

How Do you make Passive Income From Rental Property?

There are various ways to make your passive income when you buy rental properties. Let us look at the various ways to do this.

Offer Rental Property in the Neighborhood

Among the various ways to make passive income from your property is to have a rental property in the neighborhood that you stay. However, you need to follow the same procedure that you do for other investments.

While the rule of passive investments is such that you don't have to be involved in the property actively, this shouldn't be the case with new investors because you need to learn how the system works.

Offer the Service Out of the area

Another profitable method to make passive income is to establish property in another area then offer it for rent. This is ideal for experienced investors that want to take advantage of good prices out of their areas. However, you have to work with a few trusted individuals to handle the establishment.

Know What to Invest In

Many investors get attracted to bargains very fast. This shouldn't be a mistake that you make as well; you need to avoid damaged properties like the plague. Make sure that you go for a property that is in your range and it helps you get returns as fast as possible.

Opt for a Higher Down Payment

For most new traders, the notion that they can get a loan for buying a property at little or no down payment makes the prospect very attractive, and they run for these loans without wondering why other traders aren't doing the same.

Well, for your information, the lower the down payment, the higher and the interest rates to pay. You also make the repayment plan longer and more strenuous.

Locate the Property Near Institutions

If you were keen when you were in college, you had to hassle just to get an apartment near the school. Well, you can apply this to your rental income property business. The best ways to make passive income from a rental property is to establish it in an area that has high demand the whole year long. The appeal of the property is also high when the property is near public transport, downtown area, and shopping areas.

Rent Out Single Rooms

Yes, you might have a property that has houses, but frankly, you won't be able to make a lot of money out of this strategy. What you need to do in this case is to make sure that you rent out the individual rooms. This way, you maximize the profits compared to renting out the whole house.

When it comes to investing in rental real estate, you are either a novice or a seasoned investor. If you are a novice, the risk of making mistakes is high, and you need to use the services that are provided by various professionals to see your investment grow.

Let us look at some of the mistakes that inexperienced investors make and how to mitigate them.

1. Failure to Run checks on Tenants

As excited as you might be to get tenants so that you can start receiving rent, you shouldn't rush ahead of yourself to do this. The first step you need to do before accepting the tenant is to run a background check. Let the tenant fill out a form that will give you all the information.

Even if the tenant is able to pay the deposit and several months of rent, you need to hold your horses and run the checks.

2. Assuming the Property Will Always be Occupied

Before you can pay for the property, you need to make sure you can pay the mortgage even when business is bad. This is because most investors find themselves at a point where there is no one taking the property, and they are facing financial ruin.

3. Overlooking the Cost of Repairs

Many investors don't know how to estimate the cost of running repairs or performing property maintenance. This aspect is not as easy as it seems, because repairs are unpredictable.

So, you need to come up with the right rent schedule so that you cover some of the costs while making a profit at the same time.

4. Considering it As a Hobby

One of the major issues that new investors face is viewing the whole business as a hobby. You need to remember that even if you are running the business part-time, you need to make sure that you run it as a business.

One of the ways to do this is to use separate bank accounts for expenses an deposits, having a bookkeeping system and working with a tax professional to make sure you understand the taxing policy and to pay your dues.

5. Relying on Promises

When doing business, you need to stop relying on promises from the other party. For your own peace of mind and legal protection, you need to have your tenants sign an agreement when leasing the property so that you have it on file that you entered an agreement on such a date with the person.

Make sure you understand the rules that govern real estate investing in different states, and these rules make sure you follow everything to the latter.

6. Tenant Neglect

The property that you rent is your full responsibility. This is why it is vital that you involve a management company in the process so that it remains viable.

Make sure that you stick to your lane, though, because privacy is also a sensitive issue when it comes to handling tenants. Take care not to violate their privacy by entering their homes unannounced. They might end up suing you because you are violating the terms that are in the lease agreement.

7. Asking Wrong Questions

Many tenants understand their rights and will try to respond the best way possible when you take them through the screening procedure. However, they also understand the role of the law when it comes to these processes, and you need to be aware of this. Make sure you ask only relevant questions.

There are various rules that protect the tenant, and stipulate that you cannot reject clients offer on various aspects such as marital status, sex, age, color, race, family status, handicap, and religion.

8. Failure to Meet Housing Codes

By now, you must be privy to the fact that housing always needs some codes. You need to take care of various parts of the property to make sure they conform to the safety and health standards. Failure to meet the end of your bargain can lead to penalties or even lead to court cases.

9. Delaying Evictions

When you realize that the tenant is not suitable for your property, it is ideal that you start eviction procedures against him or her. If you delay the eviction and you get problems with the tenant, you will have no one to blame. So, make sure you start eviction processes early enough by contacting an attorney for any legal process.

10. Going Against Lease Terms

If you came up with lease terms and you don't enforce them, then you will fail to uphold the standards that make rental income a good way to make money.

Make sure the terms are written clearly down, and they are detailed well enough to be understood by the different parties involved. Doing this gives you evidence that you need when something comes up that requires you to show evidence. Remember for you to make something out of the various allegations that come during the investment period, you need to provide the necessary evidence.

Chapter : 4
When Is It Ideal To Engage In Passive Income?

Everyone has their Financial Situation

We come from different families and backgrounds of varied potential. This means that our financial start point is not similar. Some people come from families that already attach them to a source of income before they can finish college. These are families that own businesses. Others have to emerge from backgrounds marked with financial difficulty defy all odds and eventually enter professions to get employed. They start getting salaries sometime after college and after going out on job hunting missions. After getting jobs, they have to use the wages to settle a lot of issues in their families before they can fully focus the earnings to themselves and forge a path to financial freedom. This means that each one has their own circumstances, and hence, people have to make steps towards creating a stream of income based on the financial realities glaring at them.

However, building wealth calls for a shift in the mental and behavioral set up of a person. These impacts on the financial habits that a person has. Even when the situation of a person matters in determining the kind of economic slump they have to rise from, it is a fact to posit that everyone needs to gear their habits and mindsets to the correct targets. As a motivation, there are some notable personalities who decided to take measures to turn around their financial fortunes for the better and have ended up creating generational wealth.

Chris Reining is a case in point among those famed for how they made themselves millionaires once they decided to do what was required. He, for instance, beat the glass ceiling of reaching $1 million net worth just at the age of thirty-five years. He then retired two years later at the age of 37. He achieved this because he took the necessary steps to ensure that his finances are automated. By automating his finances, it means that he succeeded in creating a stream of passive incomes that continued to yield returns in a fountain-like manner. However, it is vital to perhaps dissect passive income by perceiving it as a financial concept.

Passive income has already been explained in previous chapters, and some people have understood it based on their own conceptions of what it is. For instance, Todd Tresidder has had a distinct practice as a wealth consultant and coach. He posits that passive wealth as the kind of earnings that is cashed in regardless of one's schedules or time factor. However, this does not presuppose it as money that one morning just picked up like one picks up letters from the mailbox. It does not only appear from the blues.

He refers to it as income that is lagged. By this, he means that all effort and time is vested in the building of a system that then like a watch or machine is left up to run by itself and churning out products that in this case is income. This explanation concurs with the fascination held by Brad Hines towards passive income. He describes that when he heard of passive income as a concept of financial freedom, he immediately was enchanted. However, he says that making it work for him proved to be a hill to climb as he tried to actualize it. However, he realized that if a person is not associated with any passive income, it means that they are wasting time since they are unable to squeeze value out of every minute of their time.

This is the essence of passive income, to ensure that every moment; the financial system that has been created is working to one's financial benefit. Every person likes to achieve freedom. This is particularly freedom from being under compulsion to work for failure to do that means no money comes in. This freedom is found in passive income. The mechanics of it is that it is not connected to time in the productive sense of it. It means that one can use their time that would otherwise be spent in productive occupation to do other things. Life becomes flexible, and one can set their own terms of life, work, and enjoyment. From the accounts of those who achieved significantly on the metrics of passive income, they say that when the earnings that are passive go up, one becomes freer from the enslavement of money. It is no longer about one going about chasing money. Money just drips in, and worries about how much less or more is in savings, or expenditures and debts just varnish away.

Talk of the Best Timing to Start

So what is the perfect time to create passive income? This question touches on the very essence of passive income. Every success story with regard to passive income shows the urgency with which actions towards financial freedom have to be made. Guaranteeing oneself an income is never about the ideal time. Expenses do not wait. When one is procrastinating and acting lazy with their time, diseases and other factors that exert pressure on one's finance do not wait. It is about realizing that every time wasted is an opportunity lost. An opportunity that could otherwise render the rest of life easier, more relaxed, and without pressure. Financial planning should start as soon as one attains the ability to perceive life and the financial implications attached to it. Once one is able to connect that money takes effort to earn, and that life is about expenditure. They take measures to cushion themselves from the pressures of active income and the rigorous burden of the need to plan expenses, savings, and other financial constraints that may make life hectic. The question of how exactly to create passive income will be addressed in the coming discourses of this paper. However, one does not appreciate the means if the rationale is not well stipulated. They have to understand the need and the urgency of it in order to understand the worth of it all.

It is not possible for a person to be thinking of financial freedom without having set up a flow of cash flow. In fact, lack of this puts one in the danger of slumping into debt. Grant Cardone is an example of people who were so much buried in debt as a result of dependence on active income. However, he says that the current income is supposed to be perceived as capital that is supposed to be invested in putting one on a path of financial freedom. He says that most of the people usually become too comfortable with active income and take it for everything that they will ever earn in their whole life. They become satisfied too quickly and stop to open their minds and realize that there are opportunities all around them. Some even own up problems and accept them as part and parcel of their lives and pass them on to succeeding generations.

Regardless of how much one gets in active income, this way of life is only a testament of an impoverished mind. Instead, to expand one's income means one is ready to engage in a "side-hustle" or just fully plunging into a side job that has earnings that are satisfactory or high enough. The point here is not to get comfortable. It is essential to keep up the pace and to always turn up the targets and dreams to the point where one starts to feel limitless.

Even when so much awareness has been realized with regard to passive income, there are still many people who are yet to get charged up and embrace it. They still are yet to appreciate the benefits that they can reap if they decided to venture out. Perhaps the critical aspect is to know why it is a big deal in modern life even more than ever before. As such, those who realized it early enough and dared it in the past when opportunities were wide open have by now distinguished themselves as by the wealth they have accumulated in the form of automatic income. People do not seem to fear discomfort much enough. Even with the sure promise of alleviating worry and discomforts, people seem to have steeled up to endure. This leads to customary poverty tolerance.

Some still think that passive does not immediately help them turn around their fortunes. They believe it is about returns in the long terms and feel that the risks are too many. Others even see the benefits as only reaped in retirement. This is not the case. In fact, passive income takes care of both the present and the future. It also alters the dynamics of one's revenue since it is not about proceeds that will come later on. With the income that is additional, it boosts the earning potential of a person. This can switch things immediately to favor the desire for some comfort. It means more disposable income available and hence, higher purchasing power. This is for the present which still can be worked out to cater to future financial plans.

It is worth pondering as well that when energies start to dwindle one will still require life to keep going as usual. Sometimes people get conditions that require them to take time off work. That should not mean that life stops all of a sudden. This can happen anytime. Accidents happen, and they can happen today or tomorrow. The question is, what if last month's active income was the last. Will life stop? Even in the absence of an accident or an incapacitating incident, no one has the infinite energy to work their whole lifetime. At the right time, people have to retire, and others have to take up the boots that the old hang. At this time, there will be no other choice but to look at the alternative sources of income. Definitely, passive income is what takes over to meet the expenses of life. Yet, no one knows how soon this time can come.

Statistically, up to 70% of the workers in the US opt out of active employment and work at the average age of 65. In fact, most of these opt for retirement years before 65. When it comes calling, everyone needs to be able to think of the way to respond. In the form of health conditions, accident, or family obligations that require close attention, it should not spell a turn of life for the worse. Passive income is, therefore, an important bridge to help cross through times that would otherwise have been of a financial downturn.

Passive Income as a Succession Plan

It is also necessary to think of ways of ensuring that future generations have something to inherit from their parents. Heirs are definitely supposed to be integrated into the financial plan. There has to be a stream of continuity in terms of cash flow longitudinally along the line of succession. The succession plan in this inclines one rather have monies streaming inadequate measure as opposed to piling up savings that could then end up being wasted away.

No one should be too young to think about their children. Most of the wealthy people always obsess about how their children will live once they are gone. They do not want their children to go through similar struggles in building their way up to the top. It should not be a case of every generation for itself such that the children also start from scratch to then develop their own path to financial freedom. Parents are supposed to lay down some form of a framework through which the following generations can start life on and be guided to even higher levels of financial achievement. This kind of planning also helps to elevate one to higher levels of thinking and inspires greater actions of investment. Assuming that there is time and indulging in the consumption of earnings as opposed to investing it can create anxiety in later years once it dawns on one that they did not plan ambitiously enough. It also appears of one to be mean, and in fact, one can be judged harshly for lack of meaning inheritance to pass down the generations.

Tax Benefits

Taxation is a sensitive aspect of income that everyone has to be aware of. This is because it cuts down earnings and sometimes so much that one feels they are working for the government. From the time someone earns their first salary, they immediately feel the taxation pinch. For active income, it is not possible for anyone to escape the sharp cutting edge of the taxman that is always waiting to chop a part of the salary. It is not something that anyone should look at with a blind eye and accustom themselves to. This is not to say that paying taxes is bad. It is partly ethical and responsible as citizens who enjoy government services. Everyone has to contribute to the duty of building the nation. However, the taxes c0omke as an obstacle to optimal earning and hence impede the ability of someone to maximize their income.

This means that the taxes that are imposed on income have to be perceived as losses of some sort. Keeping on incurring the losses on income due to tax deductions without looking for ways to recoup the deducted income is detrimental to one's ability to sustain a constant pace to financial freedom. People who understand the pinch of taxation go out of their way to create an alternative stream of income that could serve as compensation on the various cuts on their active income. This can help to remedy the pinch that one keeps feeling every time the paycheck comes with deductions on income. The best way out to compensate for such deductions on income is to create passive income.

The structure of taxation of active income has already been considered earlier. Active income is subjected to obligatory rates that are stipulated by law. These rates are non-negotiable and therefore sanctioned. Even when tax reliefs are awarded to taxpayers, this is always negligible on the part of active income and hence insignificant. However, there is a way to remedy this by creating an escape. Most of the passive income opportunities are tax-proof. This is not to say that they are completely safe from taxation. However, they are quite out of the scope of the taxman and his ability to devise a taxation system that can impose deductions. There are some passive incomes that are quite mainstream and hence are expressly taxed and in fact involve prior taxation in the form of licenses and regular statements of tax filings of compliance. However, others are aloof and do not return interest or commission through the mainstream. The advantage of this is that one's effective tax rate significantly reduces.

The effective tax rate is the amount of tax that is payable from all the income avenues of a person. When one has a single income source, their effective tax rate is high. This can even get worse, given the fact that the government reviews tax rates from time to time. In the event that the tax rates are adjusted upwards, one can experience a financial shock on their only source of income. However, creating a web of sources of income can help to create a cushion from such shock. Assuming that a person has created multiple sources of income that are majorly passive, it means that their earnings significantly increase. Given the complexity of certain passive income modes, it means that some of the earnings trickle in tax-free. With higher earnings and only one or two sources being subjected to taxation implies that one's effective tax rate goes low. The deductions that go the tax man are well compensated for.

The best time, therefore, to start creating passive income is now. This is because of the work it requires in order to build one. It has to be understood that passive income involves the investment of time and effort upfront. One is not supposed to wait until they are thirty or forty before they can make an effort. That will have wasted a lot of time. In fact, it will mean that effort will be invested at the time when, otherwise, interest, dividends, and commons would already be coming in.

It is also essential to think about what can be gained if you invested today as opposed to tomorrow. To find motivation, one can assume that a year from now, the passive income that will have been created will have started to bring in earnings. If it is an investment through shares, you could calculate the compound interest that keeps growing exponentially year after year since investment. This means that the journey to being a passive income earner starts with the ability to think big. One has to be able to see the possibilities that are lying bare right before them. These are opportunities that require the brave to dare them.

Stories of millionaires that had to build themselves and rise from the enslavement of active income and money can motivate. They realized that success comes with urgency and being precise in identifying opportunities and seizing them. They realize that they are not going to be able to be rich until they get out of the group. That as long as they continue doing things the normal ways and earning in ordinary ways, their lives will remain ordinary. They understand that life is also enjoyed more when freedom is attained in the prime of their age. They comprehend the idea of thinking big and that in thinking big, come up with ideas that drive instant action. It is about knowing that those who are wealthy do not dream about the cars in the way that others think about them; they think of being the owners of the companies that make those cars. One has to find inspiration in their mind and achieve a mentality of action.

Everyone who is earning obviously thinks about investment. Investment is not just about money. It is also about time. The time factor of investment is critical with passive income. As explained earlier, passive income eventually leads to the separation of earnings from the time factor. It is about saving one from the rush, the hustle, and the bustle. Before this is attained, time is of the essence. As earlier stated, this time has first to be invested upfront. Yet people keep procrastinating. It is not possible to think of passive income without knowing how to invest time and the ideal time to do that.

For instance, one should think of someone who has thought of building a website or blog. This is a venture that requires the investment of time. The invested time will be bound in the resultant blog and afterward, when it starts to operate, no more time will be required to be invested again even when returns will be flowing out from the blog. Being idle and no thinking about investing time now means that one will keep working and time will remain a factor that dictates their life and, in effect, their earnings.

One thing to understand about time is that it is not like money. Money can be saved for future investment. Indeed, the only reason money should be saved in order that it can be invested later on in time. This is not the same as time. Time cannot be stored or banked. If that was the case, there would have been an extension of 24 hours to 27 and seven days a week to 12, and so on. We would extend our lifetimes. However, time is a fixed commodity that can only be either used or wasted. If the time is not being used or invested, it is being wasted, and as the saying goes, there is no living to recover it. We then become subjects of time, and that is why we are hurrying to make enough money to buy a home before we get children. It is the reason for the anxiety among those who are getting to retirement without having meaningfully invested. Time is itself a resource and a harsh judge. In order to use it as a resource requires instant action. Today has to be seen as offering enough opportunities to make tomorrow better.

So then everyone wants to be successful and attain the financial heights of freedom. They want it to be said of them that they were great financial planners and that they mastered the art of utilizing time as a resource. We are all seeking to write our own story for the coming generations. We even want to inspire our children to live a life of ambition and carry on their aspirations and goals. This means that everything has to start shaping up towards that direction early. It is about understanding time and its mechanics. Going it early is the only way to beat time. Because when time runs out, nothing can turn the fortunes around for anyone. It is not even winning the lottery. Failure to achieve through financial planning cannot be atoned for by anything. It is a regret that one will have to learn to live with the rest of one's life.

It is also vital to prioritize goals and to come up with clear ways to attain them. One has to spend time and determine the goals of their life and the financial and time implications they carry. However, this cannot be realized with a mental set up of complacency and laxity. Goals usually have the time factor that is one of the most strict and unforgiving. Deadlines are key since missing one's timing could spell heck a lot of doom for good dreams. It is to envision things for then one can go out and seek for methods and strategic ways of realizing them. However, the concern here is that if time is not mastered and the goals are not time-bound, they likely will not be action bound. Yet lack of action defeats the very essence of having set the goals in the first place.

Avoid Contenting with Little

The specific ways of creating passive income will be addressed in the later chapters. However, it should be emphasized that an immediate action for financial freedom is warding off contentment with little. It is also holding deep abhorrence with a life of struggle and ensuring that one is not living on the edge of survival. Lack of action and is only due to people snoozing in their comfort zones. They do not want to dare out. They fear taking risks, and they try to make ends meet even with very little. They also pick up a life of consumerism without earning enough and mostly lack the character to save enough for their investment. The motivation here is for one to understand that financial freedom requires urgency, stepping out of contentment and realizing that rather than owning up difficult life, it is possible to navigate life to heights of success creatively. However, it is not a viable prospect to realize without brainstorming and finding the right motivation. Fixing one's mentality and appreciating that time is a limited resource that runs out is essential.

On the whole, passive income is a necessary part of the financial system of every individual. It is about realizing that active income is limited in many ways, and hence, it also limits life. This bars people from achieving their dream and living the best life they want. The risks of life and the unpredictable nature of it require automation of income. This is for the sake of feeing oneself from the bondage of work and too much hustle in order to survive. It caters for the present at the same time securing the years of the unknown. Years when health, injury, and age can take a heavy toll on the ability to participate in active income. However, planning for this requires urgency and immediate action. Starting today, rather than one year, can make the difference of hundreds of thousands of dollars in automatic revenue in 10 years due to compound interest. Then one can live life boldly, free themselves from limitations and pursue enjoyment knowing even the coming generations will appreciate and enjoy the upfront effort and time invested by previous generations.

Chapter : 5
What to Consider When Purchasing Rental Properties

Buying a rental property requires a lot of research. You definitely want to get the best options available, since this is all about making a sound investment with good returns. Before investing in any rental property, there are several aspects you need to put into consideration. Let us look at some of them:

Location of the Property

Property location is very key. Remember, it is a permanent factor that can never be changed. If you choose a property whose location is not good in terms of accessibility, security, etc., you may fail to get clients for it.

For instance, it is quite advantageous to purchase an income generating property located next to a college. This is because you will always expect new students to join the college, and get your place for accommodation. If the place is secure and easy to access, there will always be demand for your apartment. Some of the location characteristics that should cross your mind include:

- Whether it is an urban, rural or suburban area
- How far the property is from necessary facilities such as shopping centers, schools, grocery stores, and hospitals
- The demand for rental houses within the location
- If the neighborhood has the potential to grow in future
- Competition with other property owners
- The type of tenants you would want to target
- Distance from your primary residence. This is important since you may need to travel to the place once in a while. If the property is far away, you may incur a lot of cost and time commuting

Remember, your reason for purchasing a rental property is for it to remain booked all year. The location must be perfect. It is one of the most important selling features of your investment. You do not want to get a property that remains vacant most of the time. A busy property always translates to more income.

The Budget

Considering that buying a property may need a lot of cash, you must do your calculations well before making the purchase. For example, you need to understand how much money is required to acquire the property and whether you will need some additional cash to, maybe, furnish the property before renting it out. If you are getting a mortgage, then you should find out how much you will need to repay on a monthly basis and what the interest rates will be.

Property Value

Since this is an already existing property, find out from the owner the real income and expenses. Request for a sheet containing income and expense information for a number of months or years. This will give you a clear picture of how much to expect from the investment. If there is no such information, then get some values to help you predict reasonable operating costs for the property.

Make sure you calculate the net operating income (NOI) beforehand. This refers to the difference between the revenue generated from the property and the operating expenses. Most real estate investor uses the NOI to evaluate a property's cash flow and determine if it is worth investing in it. The resultant figure is also useful in determining the initial price of the property.

Also, when determining a property's value, you must get information about the vacancy rate of the location. This is the percentage of rental units that are vacant in a given area within a particular time. It helps determine the rate of demand for your new property. With this, you will also need to estimate the projected rent for your property, how much you will need to spend on insurance, tax, and maintenance.

When it comes to the property's value, the above factors and several others must be put into total consideration. For instance, you must determine the market's capitalization rate and divide it by the NOI discussed above to get the actual value of the property. The capitalization rate is used in the real estate industry to determine the rate of return expected from an investment. It is derived from the net income expected from a property. This information can be obtained from a local real estate broker. Once you have determined the values associated with the property, you will need to do an analysis of what other property owners in the area are charging their tenants so that you do not overcharge your customers.

Cost of Repairs

Identify some of the repairs you are comfortable with. State whether you need a property with mild repairs such as replacing carpets and repainting the walls, or one that has a tone of serious repairs like plumbing and wiring. Here is what you need to understand about property repairs:

- The costs vary depending on whether you are doing the repairs yourself or if you are getting an expert to do it
- Some locations have higher labor charges than others
- The cost of the repair materials may also vary depending on the value of the building. A high-quality property will need high-cost materials to repair and vice versa.
- Some repairs may cost more than the estimated amount. In some occasions, the time and budget for a repair assignment may even double. This is because, besides the repair costs, you may also incur some soft costs such as tax and insurance as the repairs are completed.

Current Market

Purchasing a property to rent it out is a good step towards financial success. If you buy a property and hold it for a good number of years, you can sell it at a profit and make a great profit from it. If you are thinking of selling the property in the future, then you must think about its resale value. Good properties are ones that can be bought and sold easily. Such are the ones that are always on demand. If you want a property for resale, then get one that has most of the features that people need. For example, people may fail to go for a property that has an in-ground pool but get one that has clean rooms and a strong structure. To appeal to most buyers, find out the important features of the property you buy, that can make people interested in it when the time of reselling it comes.

Taxes

The taxes incurred on properties will definitely vary depending on your location. Paying huge taxes for a house that is located in a busy environment is not an issue since you expect your property to be occupied all through. Talk to the municipality's office or other homeowners in the area to get any relevant tax information. It is also important to find out if there is a likelihood that the current tax will increase in the near future. This will help you decide whether to settle for the property or not.

Vacation Rentals

Vacation properties differ from ordinary rentals in so many ways. The condition of the home will determine if you will get regular tenants. It is good not to assume that your investment will remain booked all through the year, although this is possible. When getting a vacation property for renting out, get one that is within your budget. This will ensure that you remain with some extra cash to depend on within the first few years, or until the property is able to attract a steady number of tenants.

You need this extra cash to pay for the home's fixed costs such as mortgage and taxes as well as other unexpected charges for furnishing, property management, maintenance, and unexpected repairs.

Just like any other home, ensure that the location of your rental property is accessible and convenient to your target clients. Most vacation rentals are hired by non-city residents. You want a location that has several options in terms of transport. Is there a bus system nearby, does the rental have private parking? Can your guests find a car hire service nearby? Lack of access to these features can make your guests' experience a difficult one, and they may decide not to consider your home when next they visit.

You may wish to engage a real estate agent in purchasing your property; however, it is advisable that you start the search on your own. Getting an agent too early into the process may cause you unnecessary pressure and make you incur more unnecessary costs.

Finding a Profitable House to Flip

House flipping is common in real estate. It is different from purchasing of rental property as an investment since the main aim of house flipping is purchasing the property at a discount, improving on it and selling it at a profit. This is a quick-income generation strategy for real estate investors since properties are acquired at fairly low prices and sold at relatively high prices. In house flipping, there are a few aspects that determine the success of the whole process. Let us look at some of them.

- *The Basement Sales Price*

To succeed in the house flip business, you must always prepare for the worst case scenario. Find out whether there is a similar house within the property area that has sold for less than what you want to buy. If the price is lower, you should take this as the basement sales price for your flip. This amount is what will serve as your selling price for the property in case things go wrong. For example, if you purchase a flip at $500,000, and there is a similar house nearby sold at $350,000, then the later should serve as your basement sales price. However, you should strive to resell the property at a higher cost to make a profit.

- *The Pop Potential*

Once you have the basement cost set, you might need to factor in the pop potential of the flip. Real estate agents encourage investors to list some homes at a price that is somehow below the market cost. This is because a buyer may just come in and make a bid that is higher than everyone else by thousands of dollars. A property, for example, may remain listed for sale at $750,000 for over two weeks then a buyer comes and takes it at $800,000. This is a better profit that if a home was listed at a less amount and sold within days. Having a number of homes listed in the same range may make your deals go more quickly and thus raise your basement sales price.

- *The area's Near Meridian Price Range*

If your intention is to build large, nice homes within an area, then be set to lose money. This is because most people that live within that region may not be able to afford your expensive homes. A lot of people living in an average neighborhood may not be ready to buy a new house. If they are, they may not be willing to overspend. It will, therefore, be difficult to sell an expensive flip to them.

You may manage to make a sale when the market is going high, however when it declines; you may lose a lot. Avoid this by targeting properties that would sell for a price that is close to the average price range for the area or city. Consider the number of potential buyers within the region. A large number of buyers increase the potential of getting a higher bid for your flips.

- *The Value Add*

The first question you need to ask yourself before settling on a possible flip is what its story is? The truth is, you want to know if investing in such a house will give you distress or profit. For instance, a flip that has been vacant for years will have several non-functional components and appliances. The owner may be selling it quickly, and at a low price just because he or she needs the money urgently. This may be a good deal because you can add value to the house and resell it at a good price. With intensive renovation or a rebuild scenario, you can quickly make money on such a flip. If you land a good deal, always ask yourself why. It feels good to be able to explain why you have to buy a flip at a certain price and what will make you gain some profit from it.

- *The Surrounding*

This is one feature that most real estate investors forget about, yet it is as important as the rest. If you intend to acquire a house, check the condition of the other homes nearby. These do not need to be new but should be appealing enough for potential buyers to desire to live in such a surrounding. Keep off houses that look terrible unless you are planning to refurbish them before listing them for sale. Take a walk around the neighborhood and speak to some people. Ask them how the place is. Most of them will be happy and willing to share information about the place they call home, and if there be any negative comments, you can base on these to make a decision.

Rental Property Profits and ROI

In a good year, most rental properties should be able to generate at least 10% of the initial cost as revenue. As an investor, you must always calculate the amount of profit you are receiving on a monthly or annual basis as this will help determine the investment's worth. The return on investment or ROI is a measure that helps you achieve this. It measures the profit made on a property as a percentage of the investment cost.

Calculating the ROI for a rental property can be tricky, especially if the variables involved are not clear. Most people include or exclude some variables in the calculation, ending up with the wrong results. It becomes more complicated when investors are given the option to pay in cash, or when they are using a mortgage to pay for the property. Here are two formulas that you can employ when calculating the ROI.

ROI = Net Income divided by the Cost of Investment

Or

ROI = Investment Gain divided by the Investment Base

The first formula is the most common. Remember, the ROI is a ratio that represents the profit as a percentage. For example, if you buy a property at $800,000 and sell it at $900,000, then the net profit will be $100,000, and the return on investment would be $100,000/$800,000 which is 0.125

This equation works for most of the basic businesses. You must, however, note that real estate involves a number of variables that can affect the ROI ratio. These include things such as maintenance and repair costs, mortgage interests, and many more. The terms of financing a property greatly impact the cost of investment as well as the profits made from it.

ROI from Cash Transactions

In the case of purchasing a rental property using cash, the formula for calculating the ROI is quite straightforward.

Assuming that you purchase a rental property at $100,000 cash. The closing price was $1000 and the remodeling price

$9000. This means that the total amount invested on the property was $110,000. If you charge a rent of $1000 each month, you will have $12,000 in one year. This amount fewer expenses say $2400 comes to $9600. To calculate the ROI

Divide $9600, which is the annual return by the total investment made, in this case, $110,000.

To convert it to a percentage, multiply the figure by 100.

The answer is 8.7%.

ROI from Financial Transactions

If you, for example, purchase the same property by mortgage and the down payment was 20% of the purchase price, then 20% of $100,000 is $20,000. Then the closing costs went to $2500 as this is typical for mortgage sales. The remodeling costs remain the same. The total initial cost was $20000+$9000+$2500 = $31500. Other ongoing costs would be the interest rate, in this case, 4%. The monthly cost would be $581.93. With a rental income of $1000, the cash flow will be this amount minus the mortgage payment. You will remain with about 428.07 as your income.

A year later you will have $5016.84, and the ROI will be 15.9%

Rental Houses and the Market Demand

When you engage in real estate, you purchase a property and the land on which it is built. Just like any other asset business, real estate operates on supply and demand. The prices of properties depend on the law of demand and supply. High demand and low supply always result in high prices. The costs go down when there are low demand and generally high supply of homes within an area. Demand is often affected by changing lifestyles, natural disasters as well as a drop in the interest rates. Supply and demand always work against each other, until a steadiness in the price is reached. This is called equilibrium.

The housing industry depends a lot on the above law. Each real estate transaction involves a seller and a buyer. The buyer bids on a property, and the seller has a choice to accept or reject this bid. A low supply of properties causes the prices to go up. This is what causes bidding wars since several buyers may raise their offer prices in an attempt to outbid each other. This becomes advantageous to the seller, who is now able to make tremendous profits. A weak economy and a large supply of properties cause the prices to go down. Since it takes a lot of time purchasing and selling homes, the market can never be quite predictable.

One other factor that may affect the demand and supply of real estate is the drop in interest rates. When the borrowing cost or interest rates go down, people take up more debt so that they can finance their purchase. During this period, more buyers flood the industry, causing the demand to rise. If the supply is a bit low, the prices tend to go up.

Housing Market Crash

As you invest in real estate, always beware of any imminent signs of a market crash. When borrowing rates become too low, and banks relax their mortgage terms, most people who would otherwise not afford to buy homes proceed to get a house loan. These are called subprime borrowers. During this time, more buyers hit the market, causing a rise in the demand and a drop in the supply. This drives the prices too high, somehow unrealistic levels that most of the investors are unable to afford. The investors thus pull out of the market, causing a sudden drop in the demand as well as the prices within a very short time. This leads to a total collapse in the market.

Working with Real Estate Agents

With the amount of information available online today, most property buyers do not see the need to engage the services of a real estate agent. Several advertising channels are available for free and may be useful in providing all the information you need. However, there is a bigger role played by an agent than just getting you what you need. Here are some reasons why you might still think of getting one.

Expertise

With a real estate agent, you do not need to learn about anything to make a transaction successful. The agent guides you in the entire process because he knows everything about real estate buying and selling. The trick lies in finding the right person for the job. Most of them charge relatively the same fees so you should not worry about being overcharged.

Additionally, most agents will help with your property visits and showings. They keep property owners' agents at bay, thus saving you from unnecessary viewing costs. If you are a seller, the agent may help filter useless calls from reaching you and only get serious buyers to reach you.

Cost Information

A real estate agent can help you make the right choices in terms of the cost of the property. They can provide you with price negotiation strategies that work and help you get more interest in your property if you are a seller.

Besides cost information, you will also gain from their market condition information, which can help you estimate the right time to buy or sell an asset. You will get information such as median sales prices, cost of similar properties, among others. This information goes a long way in helping you determine what to do with your intended purchase.

Location Knowledge

Working with a real estate agent who is conversant with the property area can save you a lot of time and resources. Such agents know where to find the right deals and can help you compare different locations in terms of security, accessibility, and price range. Additionally, they can easily direct you to places where you can get information about amenities, tax and insurance charges, and demographics.

Paperwork

Purchase agreements may contain several pages that you need to peruse and sign. This does not include the disclosure guidelines provided by local authorities. Such agreements need a keen eye to identify clauses that may cause conflicts or rob you of your investments. A real estate agent can help you identify any compromising clauses in your purchase documents and revise them accordingly.

Networking Opportunities

Agents have a network of other professionals who provide similar services. You may need such services as the process continues and your agent can easily refer you to the best in the city. They understand the best service providers in the neighborhood and can help you negotiate prices for such services.

Assistance with Post-purchase Concerns

Once a transaction is completed, questions or concerns may arise in areas like tax collection, transfer of ownership, and so forth. A good agent will always be on standby to assist you to get answers on any questions that may pop up. They remain in constant communication should you need to make more transactions in the future. Some will go to the extent of sending you information on the best deals in town.

Tips for Getting Started

On average, the best property to invest in as a beginner is either a condominium or single-family unit. Condominiums are good for starters because they are low maintenance. In many cities, the condo management agencies take care of external repair costs and leave the buyer only to repair the interiors. In case you need to invest in a condo, be sure to note that they often attract low costs in terms of rent. The rise in cost is the slowest and mostly attracts short-term renters.

Single-family units, on the other hand, attract long-term tenants. This is because family people tend to have a stable income that is able to cover their monthly rent charges. Look for a property that has potential to grow in value in case you want to increase your cash flow in the future. Do not ignore those that seem more expensive than you can afford. This is because most properties cost lower than the listing price.

Compare prices of different properties and find out the final costs to understand what the market value is like within your location of interest.

In terms of appreciation, check for houses whose prices can shoot upwards after renovation. This is particularly important if you want to venture into house flipping or if you intend to sell the property after some years. To make a profit from a real estate investment, strive to obtain it at a reasonable cost. The recommended price for any rental property is not more than 12 times the income you expect to receive an annual basis.

Determining Rental Charges

You have acquired a rental property – how do you determine the rent charges? Be sure not to make any assumptions as you have to work the figures out based on a number of factors. If you set the rent very high, you will not attract many clients. Setting the rent too low may make potential tenants to doubt the standard of your house. Find out an average cost from the neighborhood and start from there. Make some additions or deductions depending on your mortgage repayment costs, taxes, insurance, repairs, and maintenance.

When it comes to maintenance and repairs, the cost may be high or low depending on the type of property acquired. An old house may need lots of regular repairs while a new one may only require a few or none. If you do some repairs by yourself, you may reduce the costs significantly. If dealing with a property management company, think about using only one for all your repairs. This will save you some costs as well.

Every neighborhood has good and sometimes, bad properties. It is upon you to carry out the necessary research and footwork if you want to get the best deals. Set realistic expectations for every purchase or sale you make and exercise some patience as it may take some time for you to realize any profits.

Chapter : 6
How to Maximize Rents

Every Person Should Understand That It Is Possible To Invest Money

Many people perceive the word investment as being impractical with them. They think that investment only involves big money projects into the major sectors of the economy and with a promise of huge returns. In this case, they feel intimidated with the mention of the word investor or investment and perceive it as a reserve for millionaires or those carrying home hefty packs in monthly earnings.

This is a mindset of inferiority that leads to lack of purposeful financial initiative. People are supposed to be able to make decisions that most benefit them financially. They underrate themselves and resign to a life of overreliance on the paycheck. This is the reason why people have to open their eyes and see that opportunities for investment are many. Not all investment opportunities are capital prohibitive. Some require more investment in time, commitment, and effort as opposed to the huge initial capital.

It has to be understood that the point of investment is to grow the initial capital. It is about understanding the mechanics of investment. That it grows the initial capital over time to the level where one is able to break even. The investment starts to stand on its own without requiring more channeling in sums of money from the person investing. At the breakeven point, one is able to reap back the principle which he invested and afterward start registering profits.

The reluctance to invest can also be as a result of undermining low returns. There are people who look at some investments and despise the returns. They think returns are meager and will not help them much. Yet most multinational companies count on returns that are quite low but are expanded over a large market to ensure they are sufficient. A mobile operator, for example, may just get back $2 dollars from a customer each day. But looking at the $2 dollars each day of the year makes it some good return from just one customer. In building the business, the operator then works on expanding the subscription by registering more customers on their network. It is not about looking at the $2 return. It is about the possible $ 100,000 if the customers are fifty thousand and more.

Investment has to be seen as an obligation. The income that comes from work has to be seen for what it is, mere capital. It is meant to be expanded and open up opportunities for more secondary and tertiary avenues of earning money. The only question is with regard to where the investment should be directed. Investment should be researched and follow a scheme of mentorship in order to avoid frustration and misdirecting hard-earned money into a venture whose risks can wipe away a fortune.

Essentially, therefore, every person has to be thinking about how to expand their income. Everyone has to think of ways to ensure they can beat financial woes and can rise above the tide of impoverishment. This is by constantly researching ways of enhancing earnings to a level where they no longer have to worry about expenses. They should drive themselves out of the fear to invest and know that there is an opportunity for everyone to invest at any level they are at. The high-income earners the same as the low-income earners all have to do something to ensure that their income is automated.

Investment Can Be Done Even Without Money

Investment in the economic sense of the word has a monetary connotation to it. One cannot deny that fact. However, this would mean that those without an income have been ruled out from ever having to invest. Indeed they are because many investments require a certain amount of capital. However, investors should be seen as a mentality first before action. There are so many people whose paycheck loads their accounts with cash. However, they have been unable to see beyond their paychecks and plunge into a meaningful income-generating investment.

There are others who are busy surviving on their active income and working so hard at their jobs that they have no time to focus on secondary investments that could even relieve them of the pressure at work. However, some of the investment success stories have been about people who otherwise would have been written off. Yet they embody the correct financial mentality that investment is about how one thinks. It is about what is in someone's head as opposed to what is in someone's bank account.

In this era, a lot of sources of capital exist. Governments are even giving out grants for people who want to engage in small enterprises in order to survive. As a matter of fact, governments require people to have the ability to create jobs for themselves and for others. This will relieve it of the burden of unemployment that successive regimes have to grapple with. It can always be happy to support any enterprising people who have taken up the onus to be self-employed. It would be fallacious to purport that those without an income are then condemned to a poor life. Just like a person who has money can fail to think out of the box is the same way a person without it can.

To think out of the box typically involves the willingness to understand that nothing in life is cut out in black and white. It is about focusing on the grey areas for a way out. There are people who ventured into investments with money, and then the business failed and even brought them down to their knees, consuming all their savings. They, however, still found a way to try another business and keep trying until they eventually came out of it successfully. When they went back to zero, they did not give people and think that they are useless as naught. It is about looking at one's ability to create and develop from anywhere using the available opportunities. As a matter of fact, opportunities are all around people.

In order for one to invest, they have to be creative. Creativity is the ability to devise, invent, or improvise for the purpose of making something work. To come up with investment ideas, one has to be creative. It is only through creativity that one can set themselves apart from the rest in the way they do their things. For instance, one can think of a way to make the abilities they learned in school work for them. Not all of them require capital. To create a website, for instance, is not hinged to income as much as it is on competence and understanding the website will do in order to fetch returns.

Similarly, engagements such as freelancing are opportunities that do not require an investment of capital. Only time and money are required together with one's ability to draw on his competencies and get the work done. There are a dozen of other investments that only require access to a gadget such a smartphone, laptop, or tablet to set up something that can work. This is the reason why investors should not be mistaken as totally capital reliant. Even if it is, there are avenues that have been set to circumvent that hurdle through micro-finance, grant, and even borrowing from well-wishers. Honestly, it should not be absolutely impossible to find support for an investment idea that is plausible and worthwhile.

Renting to investors

Renting is one of the passive income avenues that people can take advantage of. This is because of the numerous ways that one go around it. Renting has opportunities for all. It starts from the real estate development that is a big money affair to the other rental investments that require low capital. However, real estate investment has a lot of other windows in which one can participate at their level of economic muscle to generate wealth.

Rents do not just involve in being a property owner alone. The way to invest in rents is quite similar to the ay that people usually select from among the many specialties in the medical field. People only dreamt that they would love to be a doctor but initially had no idea a doctor or what. Then you realize later than in this field, specialties are numerous and some of which were, to one, unheard of.

Only after focusing on research, becoming more interests and digging deeper is when one realizes what specialty best suits them. This is akin to the situation with real estate investment and income on rents. It not to worry and shy away in inferiority. Instead, one has to come out and research to realize the various niches that can be a target for investment and deciding which one to take an interest in with due respect to the requirements needed.

The niches in renting can start with ownership, as highlighted earlier. Ownership can be in partnership or as a sole proprietor. There are ways to do it even and become an owner if sole ownership is way out of one's financial reach. For instance, syndication can help people with limited abilities join together and ensure cut a deal for ownership of a property for rental purposes. In syndication, one sponsor or operator arranges for an agreed number of people to buy a property where each partner can have limited rights and purchase shares of the total value of the property.

The value of properties depends on the kind of property. This is whether it is a single-family unit, duplex, apartments, or other. In the case of an apartment, syndication works by the investors pulling resources together under the umbrella of the sponsor or operator who does all the work of organizing the project. All those with shares in the arrangement are then enrolled for dividends that are disbursed on either a quarterly or monthly basis. It is then the duty of the operator to ensure value addition on the project by organizing management that is good. The aim is to eventually have the building sold in the space of between 3-7 years, ensuring that all partners net a profit on the basis of the share held at the end.

There are simpler rental opportunities today, for instance, in the case where one's house has extra rooms that are not used. Assuming the property is at an attractive location where people covetously would be willing to put up. One can net rental income with good profits by renting out the unused room. In the case of a good residential suit, one can earn more by turning them into per night bookings, particularly if there are factors that can make the property attractive for motel-like investment. This kind of rent is a gamble, but when it works, it can lead to unintended profits and bring passive income.

In other arrangements, one can get more creative o to ensure they are earning dividends in the rental sector. For instance, one could find a rental property deal for use by tourists or such other utility. In order to ensure professionalism in running it, the property can then be transfer to investment professionals in the line business. They can run the business and market it and ensure that the deal includes in one sharing part of the income. This can be really interesting and exciting if the deal is struck with clear terms. The terms should totally place management expenses and operational costs on the business operators and only wait for the profits that come in the form of passive income.

What this demonstrates is that investment in renting is not all about the ability to afford things and procure them by one's own financial capacity. It is a field where one can apply creativity and earn back returns. One can even diversify and combine multiple avenues of rental income. It all depends on the ability of an individual to think out of the box and improvise. What could seem like a useless idea could shockingly turn into a robust rental income?

Thinking Outside the Box

It is necessary for all people to understand that investment is only possible where thoughts and creativity are well directed. It is about the willingness to identify opportunities, even in the places that others would otherwise see none. This is particularly the case for those who are seeking avenues of investment yet do not have the huge income packs to raise thousands of dollars in capital. These opportunities can be found both online and offline. It just takes the willingness to research, explore, and dare.

Talking of willingness to think outside the box, one wonders if people could trust investment with an initial investment capital of $500. Companies such as Fundraise have come up with the idea that helps those who are interested in investing but do not have huge capital. This company invests in the real estate sector. It does this without requiring investors to assume the position of landlords or trying to be a landlord.

In this arrangement, money collected from various people who have invested in the project is appropriated into separate portfolios. This is not, however, hidden from investors as information is shared as to which portfolio one's money has been placed. The portfolios are about financing various real estate projects around the USA.

It will operate essentially like stock such that profits emerging from the investments in the projects are paid out to shareholders in the form of dividends. The payments are on a quarterly basis from interest accumulation and rent among other property incomes of the portfolios. It demonstrates one of the unconventional ways of generating income through investment with minimum initial capital.

The reason why there has to be thinking outside of the box is that investments involve a certain level of risk. The Fundraiser one also has its own risks, and that is why not everyone has the temerity to try it out. It requires then that anyone investing brainstorms on the ways to stay afloat in case the business does not behave in the manner that is expected. This includes looking for loopholes in the design of such an investment that one could take advantage of in order to minimize risk and maximize income.

There are various opportunities that some businesses also create for customer loyalty and promotion that a lot of people treat casually. They can also serve as a very good avenue to bolster income or at least ease up on the strap of expenses that one could be feeling quite tight on them. There, however, are more advanced programs in the digital world that could help to cash-back on shopping.

Some developers have designed cash-back apps that run on smartphones and other digital gadgets. They allow people to earn back in the same way that credit cards have been cashing back for promotional interests. An example of one of the shopping cash-back apps is Ebates. It is attached to shopping on Amazon and has been giving out some good bonuses and cash-backs. To take advantage of it, one could become creative.

This is by creating a purchase zone where a network of converges to for those seeking to make purchases. They place orders, and the zones place them online on behalf of those who have no time to make them. In the end, it becomes possible to use other people's orders to shop and cash-back on them. This is not as much passive as it involves dedication of time to create a network and popularize the service. However, it still will require thinking well to refine the idea and make it worthwhile and able to stand up as a salable brand.

In order to be able to think outside the box, someone also needs to understand well what they are good at. It can be a good investment if one delves into a venture that they could control themselves. This is in order that one can be accountable to themselves. When entering a business where one is not in control of factors, it can be frustrating sometimes staying obscured from what is happening. This is amid the pressure of one's own expectations.

The luckiest person in the investment world is the one who is handling something they love to do. This is because they are more motivated to do it. Even when frustrations come, it does not easily kill the internal drive to succeed. If anything, difficulties only trigger the ingenuity to come up with ways to keep going and make the venture work. It is therefore imperative that among the investments that one engages in, one involves being hands one or a few entail being hands-on and being among the bosses who control it.

It can be difficult to maneuver in a venture that is not one's interest area. This is because it will require hiring professionals and at startup, this will mean one immediately becomes an employer incurring wage bill expenses. This may not be plausible if one does not have the required finances to make a venture that is just starting work when it has to be complicated and involve multiple players from the onset.

However, the best part of thinking big is execution. This is the conception of the exact way that an idea will be implemented with a clear focus on the results. Some of the companies that are currently doing good business like Uber and the iPhone came out of thinking big. It was creative thought. However, what even made the ideas better is the execution. More time should be dedicated to thinking of how to make an idea work. In as much as investments and opportunities are time-bound, one should not be in a rush. Investment is not easy. It should not be done with a clouded mind, either by a promise of profits or overconfidence.

The Way to actualize Ideas

There are various ways to actualize ideas, especially in rental income. First, it is about successfully thinking outside the box and identifying the ideal investment to delve in. it then follows that the mechanics of the investment have to be analyzed, and this starts with conducting a reality check. The reality check is what leads to an accurate understanding of the kind of investment being made. All the misconceptions about it have to be mapped out. At this level, one should even seek advice from someone who has walked a similar investment path.

Listening to advice from those who experienced it first-hand can serve as a wakeup call to certain truths about an investment. It will rid the investment process off unnecessary haste and over-excitement. It needs to sink into one's had that the investment is concrete as opposed to the abstract decision that has potential fortune-changing repercussions both on the positive and adverse sides.

In conducting a reality check in rental income investment, the focus should be on the value. One has to see whether doing all that has to be done in order to make the business work or to eventually plunge into a real estate venture will bring back the worth. This value has to be directly related to one's goals of financial planning. Some returns may not really be direct or may be paid with terms that are not comfortable.

Second of all, it is about the sustainability of the rental income. Rental income is supposed to last for a long time since it involves extensive financial, time, and/or effort investment. The investments that may go into it may take a long time to save. This means that the returns from it should equally cover a long compensating while to realize the value. Income from rents is supposed to be passive income, and this should be sustainable on the large part and give one a break from the hustle.

A bad investment in real estate and rentals is that which does not have the characteristics to turn into automated income. For instance, if the income does not have the ability to generate cash flow on a regular basis, it is not worth it. If the income also varies so much, particularly by dropping significantly as opposed to sustaining a relatively predictable pattern or structure, it is a risky venture and can lead to serious losses. Even more concerning is whether the principle that is invested in the rental income will be recovered in order for one to breakeven.

One of the good things about rents as a form of passive income; however, is its ability to guarantee sustainability. Being a landlord, for instance, is a pretty guarantee that the property cannot be lost unless through a catastrophe. However, having set up some rental units or invested in a collaborative share-based real estate venture, the terms of income and the structure are clearly spelled, and one is able to understand what they will be reaping at clear intervals. The safety of this is that once one investment is successfully set up, one can disassociate with it and focus on creating a stream of other investments.

Additionally, rental income is better since it has many avenues of collaborating. Many people are interested in this are due to the promise of guaranteed income. It means that it is not a totally capital prohibitive venture. It also means that one can ride on the knowledge of the partners who share similar financial interests to ensure that everything works out well. This is as opposed to a venture that may not work well in collaboration and in which all the knowledge, effort, and capital input have to be done by the personal investment.

Just like the profits in an investment that has doors for collaboration is distributed, so are the risks. Rental income that involves partnered investment also distributes the risks among all that are involved. This cushions one from the shocks of plummeting profitability or in times of hardship in the business. However, this should be done with caution as some partners may be domineering and prove smarter to the rest. It should caution that collaboration to be based on binding agreements of how decisions are made and stipulate the interplay among all that are involved.

However, investors should not be just tied to rental income only. This income should supplement other incomes that are related to it. For instance, one could be involved in a partnership that results in the purchasing of a commercial building at a prime location. Talking of thinking big, one can then negotiate to forfeit the interests and income from the property with the occupation of some space of it without having to pay rent himself. This can be a smart way to create a tertiary investment in real estate and expand one's income by maneuvering in the rental sector.

In the end, investment should be done in a sector that is forgiving allows someone to be patient without fearing for losses. In some sectors, investment should immediately follow that one starts to get back returns. Anything other than that means that costs go up and start to eat up capital and even threaten the very business. This is not so much the case with rental income. One can invest in the purchase of property and still wait some while before it is rented away or meaningful interests start accruing. However, one does not have to develop chills that they will lose money or waste away their capital.

On the whole, everyone has to invest. There is no excuse for living a life of overreliance on the paycheck. This only leads to difficulty in saving as one adopts a hand to mouth style of life. This makes it difficult to deal with expenses, and one does not easily avoid debts that further leads to a life of worry. However, investment frees up a person as one opens up multiple channels of income. One sees more possibility in life, becomes more hopeful satisfied and therefore happier. Besides, investment better secures the future and offers a promise of better days to come.